GREEN A.

the complete guide on everything
you need to know about the green
anole

Thomas Hylthon

Table of Contents

CHAPTER ONE

INTRODUCTION

Green Anole (Anolis carolinensis)
The most generally kept and
inescapable of all types of Anolis,
the green anole, indigenous
toward the southern United States,
has been well known in the pet
exchange since the 1950s. With a
dorsal layer of lime to emerald
green (uncommon and exquisite
examples are colored blue) and
having an energetic, pinkish
dewlap (complemented in the
guys, diminished in the females),
the green anole is a dexterous

climber and intense visual tracker of arachnids, grasshoppers and other creepy crawly prey. Green anoles are amiable little reptiles that appear to appreciate being hand-taken care of, and they can make extraordinary "starter" reptiles for youthful and starting specialists. All things considered, they do have some particular consideration necessities.

CHAPTER TWO

CHARACTERISTICS OF GREEN ANOLE

The green anole breeds from March to September. The male will set up a domain and watch it. He will pull in females by puffing out his dewlap. He mates with females in his general vicinity and forcefully shields his region from different guys. At the point when a female and male mate, the female stores the sperm. In the event that she doesn't mate with another male, the put away sperm will treat her eggs. The female lays a solitary egg and covers it in soggy leaf litter, empty logs or the dirt. She will lay one egg like clockwork during rearing season. She may lay up to 15-18 eggs throughout the late spring. The female doesn't remain with the egg or care for the youthful that will incubate in five to seven weeks. Youthful green anole eat little bugs like mealworms, leafy foods flies and termites. On most green anole, the eyes are encircled by a flimsy turquoise fringe. The green anole is typically splendid green, yet it can change its shading to tanish green or dim earthy colored in a moment or two.

It is some of the time call the American chameleon since it can change shading, yet it's anything but a genuine chameleon. The green anole changes shading on account of changes in temperature, mugginess, wellbeing and disposition, not to mix into its experience. Guys have a pink or red throat fan or dewlap.

CHAPTER THREE

GREEN ANOLE BEHAVIOR AND TEMPERAMENT

Anoles can be kept alone or in little gatherings. Guys are regional and may show and battle with each other, so a gathering is best made out of females without any than one male. They are wonderful enough pets, however their characteristic nature is to secure their domain. Guys will attempt to show strength by stretching out their dewlaps to seem bigger to planned mates. In the event that it opens and shuts its dewlap, this is an indication of animosity and signs that the creature is feeling dangerous or undermined.

These reptiles are some of the time called American chameleons, in spite of the fact that they are false chameleons by any means. Anoles can change their shading from earthy colored to splendid emerald green, and they are alluring little reptiles. Guys have a pink or red dewlap (the overlap of skin under the jawline/neck), which they streak during regional and romance showcases. Females of certain species additionally have dewlaps, despite the fact that they are commonly littler and not showed as frequently. Green anoles are touchy and modest, however with steady and delicate taking care of, they will turn out to be to some degree tame. Anoles are dynamic little reptiles that hurry about rapidly, making them difficult to get. They favor not to be taken care of something over the top; keep away from it assuming there is any chance of this happening, and consistently handle them tenderly. Never hang green anoles by the tail, as anoles can confine and drop their long tail as a protection against predators in nature. At the point when an anole drops its tail, it will typically recover, however won't look equivalent to it did initially.

CHAPTER FOUR

LODGING THE GREEN ANOLE

A suitably measured aquarium with a tight-fitting screen top makes the best home; an outright least tank size would be a 10-gallon aquarium for a couple of anoles, however bigger is better and essential for gatherings of at least three. These reptiles are mostly diurnal (dynamic during the daytime) and keeping in mind that they like to loll in the sun, they like to do as such among plants. The cushions on the bottoms of their feet permit them to climb and stick to most surfaces, including glass, and they will get away from nooks that are not secure. The favored substrates incorporate soil (without perlite), peat greenery, or orchid bark.

Moistness : Utilize a hygrometer inside the nook to quantify the relative moistness; as hygrometer readings can change with age, they can likewise be adjusted once every year. Keep up the mugginess for this anole nook at 70 percent by clouding day by day with dechlorinated or packaged (not refined) water. A dish of a similar water ought to likewise be given.

Warmth : Basically, a semi-tropical condition ought to be made (not a downpour woodland) with daytime temperatures of 75 to 82 F for 12 to 14 hours out of every day. The temperature ought not fall under 65 F around evening time. During the day, a relaxing territory with a luxuriating light should cover just 25 percent of the outside of the fenced in area; focus on a lounging temperature of 85 to 90 F during the daytime. Try not to utilize hotrocks as warmth sources as they can consume your pet and furthermore end up over-warming the whole nook.

Light : An assortment of lights are required, some for heat, some for white light, and some for UVB light. Green anoles by and large need 12 to 14 hours of light and 10 to 12 hours of dimness. Mood killer all light sources around evening time. No fake light is comparable to daylight for giving UVB, so when the external temperature on a bright day is more than 70 F, place your anole outside in a safe screen or wire confine with a locking entryway. Give some shade and a concealing spot inside the bright day fenced in area.

In the event that an anole doesn't approach splendid daylight, ZooMed's reptile or iguana lights, and Durotest's Vita-Lite are two acceptable alternatives; these UVB light sources ought to be supplanted like clockwork. Glass confines, even those with a screen top, ought to never be utilized almost a window as they will trap warm and can cause lethally high temperatures.

CHAPTER FIVE

FOOD AND WATER

Anoles typically get 100% of their water admission by licking beads off of leaves of plants, so give a few plants in the nook; branches for lolling are likewise fundamental. For the most part, anoles won't lap water from a dish except if it is furnished with a steady moderate dribble, so their terrarium plants ought to be clouded twice day by day. Green anoles do best on an assortment of gut-stacked bugs including mealworms and wax worms. Feed a few properly estimated prey things, about a large portion of the size of the anole's head, each other day. A calcium and nutrient enhancement ought to likewise be cleaned on the bugs. Be cautious in permitting your anole to get wild creepy crawlies; it is highly unlikely to realize what sorts of pesticides wild-got bugs might be holding.

CHAPTER SIX

REGULAR HEALTH AND BEHAVIOR PROBLEMS

In the same way as other reptiles, green anoles are defenseless to an affliction called mouth decay or stomatitis. On the off chance that you notice puffiness or redness around its mouth or a substance that seems as though curds around its teeth, it's probably mouth decay. Try not to attempt to treat this forceful contamination with a home cure. This condition requires treatment by a veterinarian who has ability in treating reptiles. This difficult condition can prompt tooth misfortune and inevitably taint the reptile's jaw. Thus, mouth decay can be deadly whenever left untreated. Metabolic bone malady, which originates from a less than stellar eating routine or absence of UVB presentation, shows side effects of weight reduction, puffy face, and general shortcoming and laziness. Amending the eating routine and presenting your anole to a satisfactory measure of UVB beams should help.

Different reptiles are inclined to respiratory diseases; these are generally remarkable in green anoles, nonetheless, they do happen. On the off chance that your anole is wheezing or holding its mouth open, these are indications of a respiratory contamination, normally coming about because of lacking stickiness or an inadequate warmth angle in its nook. On the off chance that your anole isn't turning green and gives off an impression of being a dull earthy colored shading, this might be a sign it is focused or that it has a fundamental medical problem. Talk with your veterinarian before attempting to treat your anole at home.

Recall that all reptiles are regular transporters of Salmonella microorganisms, so legitimate cleanliness is essential when taking care of them and cleaning their hardware, particularly if kids or individuals with debilitated insusceptible frameworks live in a similar house.

CHAPTER SEVEN

PICKING YOUR GREEN ANOLE AND INTRIGUING GREEN ANOLE FACTS

Most anoles accessible in pet stores are wild-gotten. At times, pet store anoles will be got dried out and anorexic when bought, as confirmed by free creases of skin. On the off chance that a hostage reproduced reptile can be obtained, this is best, as they will in general be less focused and not as inclined to ailment or ailment.

Green anole is a sort of reptile that has a place with the group of iguanas. It tends to be found in the southeastern pieces of North America. Green anole occupies swamps, forests, parks, yards and other muggy, forested territories. Homegrown felines and over-gathering from the wild (because of pet exchange) are significant dangers for the endurance of green anoles in nature. Fortunately, populace of green anoles is still enormous and stable and they are not on the rundown of jeopardized creatures.

* Green anole is little reptile that can arrive at 5 to 8 creeps long. Guys are bigger than females.

*Green anole is brilliantly green hued, yet it effectively changes the shading into earthy colored, yellow or dark relying upon the mind-set, temperature and stickiness. Guys have pink or red fold of skin, called dewlap, on the throat.

*Green anole has versatile eyelids and its eyes move separately, autonomous from one another.

*Green anole has restricted, pointed head, slim body, long rear legs and dainty tail.

*Green anole invests the vast majority of its energy in the trees (semi-arboreal creature). It has wide cushions secured with infinitesimally little bristly projections on their feet which encourage development along the tree trunks, dividers and other vertical surfaces.

*Green anole is diurnal creature (dynamic during the day). At the point when it doesn't chase, it lolls in the sun.

*Green anole is a flesh eater (meat-eater). Its eating regimen comprises of arachnids, flies, crickets, moths, ants, termites and worms. Green anole chases just prey that is moving.

*Green anoles are regional creatures. Guys possess an area of 3 square yards. During the battles for strength, guys blow up their throat, erect peak on their backs, uncover dewlap and position themselves sideways to seem bigger.

*Green anoles likewise perform pushups and sway their heads to scare contenders. They are forceful and prepared to assault even their own appearance in the mirror.

*Principle predators of green anoles are winged animals of prey, felines and snakes.

*In the same way as other different types of reptiles, green anoles can disconnect their tail from the remainder of the body to escape from the hands or the mouth of the predator.

*Mating period of green anoles keeps going from March to October. Guys uncover their clearly shaded dewlaps to draw in females.

*Female produces 15 to 18 eggs for each season. She lays one egg at regular intervals into the home made in the empty logs, leaf litter or in the ground. Hatching of eggs keeps going 5 to 7 weeks.

*Youthful green anoles are left all alone from the snapshot of birth. They arrive at sexual development at 8 years old to 9 months.

*Green anole can endure 2 to 3 years in the wild and as long as 7 years in the bondage.

THE END

Made in the USA
Monee, IL
10 April 2021